Learning to Read, Step by Step!

Ready to Read   Preschool–Kindergarten
• big type and easy words • rhyme and rhythm • picture clues
For children who know the alphabet and are eager to begin reading.

Reading with Help   Preschool–Grade 1
• basic vocabulary • short sentences • simple stories
For children who recognize familiar words and sound out new words with help.

Reading on Your Own   Grades 1–3
• engaging characters • easy-to-follow plots • popular topics
For children who are ready to read on their own.

Reading Paragraphs   Grades 2–3
• challenging vocabulary • short paragraphs • exciting stories
For newly independent readers who read simple sentences with confidence.

Ready for Chapters   Grades 2–4
• chapters • longer paragraphs • full-color art
For children who want to take the plunge into chapter books but still like colorful pictures.

STEP INTO READING® is designed to give every child a successful reading experience. The grade levels are only guides; children can progress through the steps at their own speed, developing confidence in their reading.

Remember, a lifetime love of reading

To Josh Perl, with a mighty roar! —E.S.P.

To Patricia Scott. Thank you for your kindness and support and for keeping these dinosaur arms from going extinct. —M.S.

Acknowledgments: The author and editor gratefully acknowledge the help of paleontologists Dr. Thomas R. Holtz, Jr., Dept. of Geology, University of Maryland, and Dr. Karen Chin, Dept. of Geological Sciences and Museum of Natural History, University of Colorado, Boulder; and Marlon Janzen of the Royal Saskatchewan Museum. Thank you very much!

Photograph credits: Front and back cover: Getty Images/Leonello Calvetti; p. 3: Getty Images/ MR1805; p. 4: Getty Images/Leonello Calvetti; p. 8: Getty Images/Mark Garlick; p. 9 (top): Getty Images/ Urgurhan; p. 9 (bottom): Getty Images/Roger Harris/Science Photo Library; p. 12: Getty Images/ Rkristoffersen; p. 13: Getty Images/Mark Garlick/Science Photo Library; p. 16: Getty Images/CoreyFord; p. 17: some rights reserved by Wilson44691, found on Wikimedia Commons; p. 20: image courtesy of the Royal Saskatchewan Museum; p. 21: Getty Images/Joseph Nettis; pp. 24–25: Getty Images/Corey Ford/Stocktrek Images; pp. 28–29: Getty Images/SCIEPRO; pp. 32–33: Getty Images/CoreyFord; pp. 36–37 (top): some rights reserved by Durbed, found on Wikimedia Commons; pp. 36–37 (bottom): some rights reserved by Fred Wierum, found on Wikimedia Commons; p. 37: Getty Images/ Danefromspain; p. 40: Getty Images/Sergey Krasovskiy/Stocktrek Images; p. 41: Getty Images/ Warpaintcobra; p. 44 (left): Getty Images/Sumiko Scott; p. 44 (right): Getty Images/Daniela Duncan; p. 45 (top): Getty Images/Suma Hegde; p. 45 (bottom): CoreyFord/Stocktrek Images.

Visit us on the Web!
StepIntoReading.com
rhcbooks.com

Educators and librarians, for a variety of teaching tools, visit us at RHTeachersLibrarians.com

Library of Congress Cataloging-in-Publication Data
Names: Perl, Erica S., author. | Slack, Michael H., illustrator.
Title: Truth or lie: dinosaurs! / by Erica S. Perl; illustrations by Michael Slack. Other titles: Dinosaurs | Step into reading. Step 3 book.
Description: New York: Random House, [2019] | Series: Truth or lie | Series: Step into reading, step 3. | Audience: Ages 6–8.
Identifiers: LCCN 2018035735 | ISBN 978-0-525-57882-6 (pbk.) | ISBN 978-0-525-57883-3 (lib. bdg.) | ISBN 978-0-525-57884-0 (ebook)
Subjects: LCSH: Dinosaurs—Miscellanea—Juvenile literature.
Classification: LCC QE861.5 .P475 2019 | DDC 567.91—dc23

Printed in the United States of America
10 9 8 7 6 5 4 3

STEP 3

READING ON YOUR OWN

STEP INTO READING®

A SCIENCE READER

TRUTH or LIE
DINOSAURS!

by Erica S. Perl

illustrations by Michael Slack

Random House  New York

Hi! I'm the TRUTH SLEUTH.
I love dinosaurs!
Check out this spike-spined
Spinosaurus.
It hunted for
fish and turtles,
and even other dinosaurs.

It's TRUE!

But I smell a LIE nearby.

Let's play TRUTH OR LIE

and find it!

When you turn the page,

you'll see four statements . . .

BUT only three are TRUE.

Let's get out of here!

Which one is a LIE?

1. Triceratops was a herbivore, which means it ate only plants.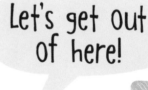

2. "Triceratops" means "dinosaur that liked to try new foods."

3. Triceratops had three horns.

4. Triceratops was able to fight the taller and heavier Tyrannosaurus and win.

Let's get out of here!

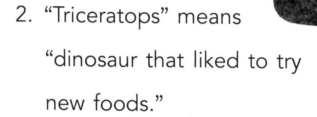

The lie is #2!

"Triceratops" means "dinosaur that liked to try new foods."

What the name means is "three-horned face."
Triceratops was a plant-eating herd animal.
But in a fight, watch out!

Triceratops could
take down larger dinosaurs,
including the ferocious
Tyrannosaurus.

1. Tyrannosaurus had about sixty teeth.

2. Some Tyrannosaurus teeth were nine inches long.

3. Tyrannosaurus's skull measured about five feet long.

4. The closest living relative of Tyrannosaurus is the alligator.

9"

60 TEETH

5'

Season's Greetings

The Gator family

11

Roar if you chose #4 as the lie!

**The closest living relative
of Tyrannosaurus is the alligator.**

Tyrannosaurus's toothy jaws
might remind you
of an alligator's.
But guess what!
T. rex is more closely related
to chickens!
Still, T. rex was no "chicken"
when it came to battles.

ROAR

Oh, my. What a big LIE!

1. All dinosaurs had teeth.

2. Some dinosaurs used their teeth
like knives for cutting through meat.

3. Some dinosaurs used their teeth like spears for catching fish.

4. Some dinosaurs used their teeth like rakes for stripping leaves off plants.

The lie is #1.

All dinosaurs had teeth.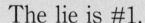

Some types of dinosaurs,

like Gallimimus and Ornithomimus,

were totally toothless!

Others, like Limusaurus,

were born with teeth

but did not grow new ones

when their baby teeth

fell out.

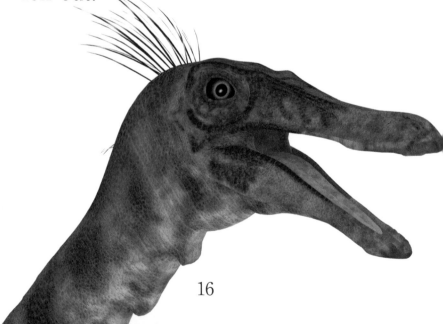

Toothless dinosaurs
and plant-eating dinosaurs
that lacked grinding teeth
swallowed gastroliths
(or "stomach stones")
to help them
digest their food.

1. One way to study dinosaurs is to examine coprolite.

2. Coprolite is the scientific term for fossilized poop.

3. The coprolite of meat-eating dinosaurs has an unusual scent.

4. Coprolite can contain fossilized beetles that made their homes in it.

Did you guess the lie is #3?

The coprolite of meat-eating dinosaurs has an unusual scent. LIE

Fossilized dinosaur poop,
or coprolite,
does provide valuable clues
about dinosaurs' lives,
including their eating habits.

Luckily for scientists,

coprolite is

so old and dry

that it does not smell

at all!

Could there be a big LIE here?

1. Sauroposeidon was
   longer than two school buses.
2. Sauroposeidon was
   as tall as three giraffes.
3. Sauroposeidon had many
   predators.
4. The first Sauroposeidon fossils
   were mistaken for
   fossilized tree trunks.

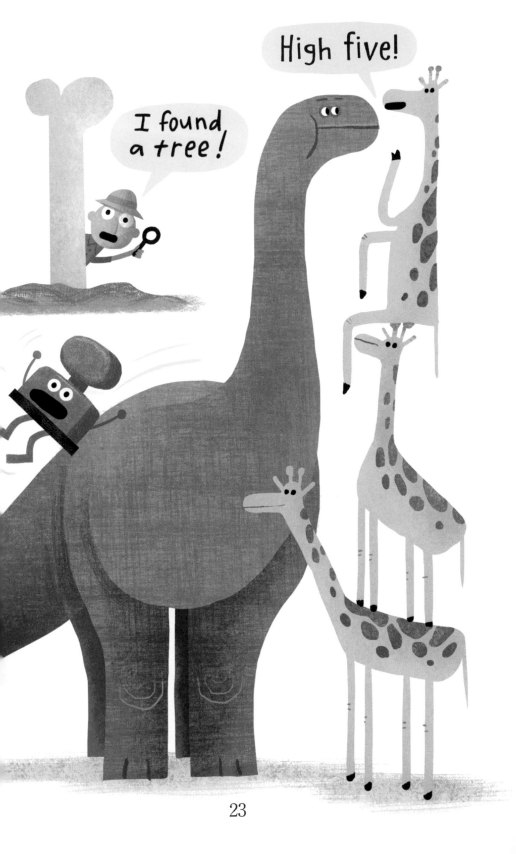

The lie is #3.

Sauroposeidon had many predators.

Sauroposeidon
did *not* have many predators.
That's because Sauroposeidon
was so big.
How big?
Up to 110 feet long.

1. Stegosaurus had seventeen armored plates on its back.

2. Stegosaurus had a brain the size of a pea.

3. The word "Stegosaurus" means "roof lizard."

4. Stegosaurus had tail spikes that were two to three feet long.

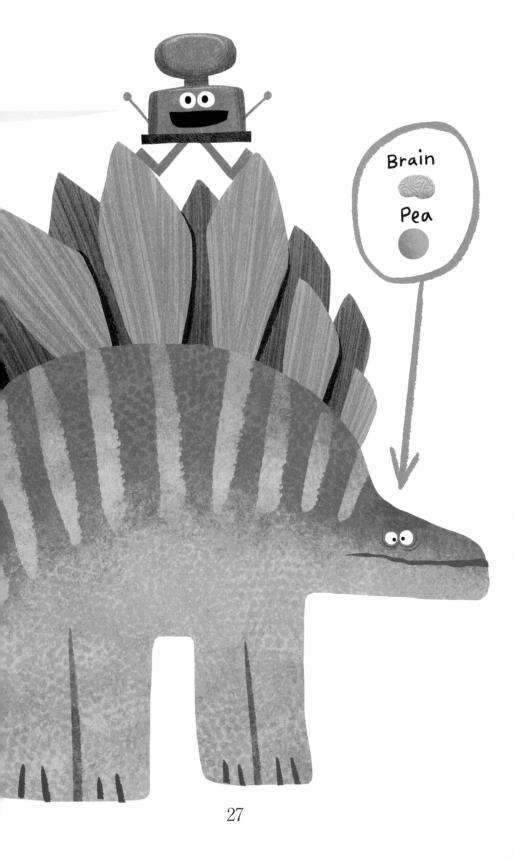

Brain

Pea

The lie is #2, Einstein!

**Stegosaurus had a brain
the size of a pea.**

It may be tempting
to call Stegosaurus
a pea-brain.
But Stegosaurus had a brain
about the same size as
a small dog's.

Stegosaurus weighed
about 6,800 pounds.
For an animal that big,
Stegosaurus's brain
was still pretty small.

LIE alert! Can you find it?

1. "Ankylosaurus" means "fused lizard."

2. Ankylosaurus is one of the largest armor-plated dinosaurs ever discovered.

3. Large plates protected
   most of Ankylosaurus's body,
   but its belly was exposed.
4. Ankylosaurus was able to run
   thirty miles per hour.

You can do it!

If you guessed #4, you're right!

Ankylosaurus was able to run thirty miles per hour.

Computer models show
that Ankylosaurus
could probably only run about
six miles per hour.
Ankylosaurus looked
like an armored tank
but moved more
like a turtle!

1. Velociraptors were the size of turkeys.
2. Velociraptors had scaly bodies, like reptiles.
3. Velociraptors could not fly.
4. "Velociraptor" means "speedy thief."

The lie is #2!

Velociraptors had scaly bodies, like reptiles.

Real velociraptors,
unlike those in the movies,
were covered with feathers.
It's true that
they could not fly.

Their arms were
too short for flying.
But their sharp claws
were perfect for
attacking prey!

Yikes! A LIE about spikes?

1. Some kinds of dinosaurs had spikes on their bellies.

2. Some kinds of dinosaurs had spikes on their backs.

3. Some kinds of dinosaurs had spikes on their tails.

4. Some kinds of dinosaurs had spikes on their front feet (like thumbs).

HUG?

39

The lie is #1!

Some kinds of dinosaurs had spikes on their bellies.

Many dinosaurs
had sharp, protective spikes
on their bodies.
Some, like Stegosaurus,
had tail spikes.
Gastonia had tail spikes
and shoulder spikes.

And Iguanodon
had spikes like thumbs
on its front feet.
No dinosaurs had
belly spikes, though.
This made even
the toughest dinosaurs
vulnerable to attacks!

Would you believe there's still one more LIE to find?

1. Bees have been around since dinosaur times.

2. Lions have been around since dinosaur times.

3. Horseshoe crabs have been around
since dinosaur times.

4. Birds have been around
since dinosaur times.

That's right—the lie is #2.

**Lions have been around
since dinosaur times.**

Bees and horseshoe crabs
have been around
since dinosaur times . . .
or maybe earlier!

And at a bird feeder, you can meet some living relatives of Archaeopteryx and other dinosaurs!

- Read with an eye for TRUTH
  and a nose for LIES.
- Share what you know
  and how you figured out
  it was TRUE.
- Play TRUTH OR LIE with your
  friends and family.

Want to Learn More FACTS About Dinosaurs?

Books to read:

Dinosaurs by Dr. Thomas R. Holtz, Jr. (Random House
   Children's Books, 2007)

Everything Dinosaurs by Blake Hoena with Paul Sereno
   (National Geographic Children's Books, 2014)

Feathered Dinosaurs by Brenda Z. Guiberson
   (Henry Holt, 2016)

Jurassic World Dinosaur Field Guide by Dr. Thomas R.
   Holtz, Jr., and Dr. Michael Brett-Surman (Random House
   Children's Books, 2015)

Websites to check out:

amnh.org/dinosaurs

amnh.org/explore/ology/paleontology

kids.nationalgeographic.com/animals/hubs/dinosaurs-and
   -prehistoric

nhm.ac.uk/discover/dino-directory